UNDER THE MOON AND STARS

A STORY BY SCOTT EMERSON / ILLUSTRATED BY HOWARD POST

GIBBS·SMITH
P
PUBLISHER

SALT LAKE CITY

98 97 96 95   10 9 8 7 6 5 4 3 2 1

Text copyright © 1995 by Scott Emerson

Illustration copyright © 1995 by Howard Post

This is a Peregrine Smith Book, published by
Gibbs Smith, Publisher
P.O. Box 667
Layton, Utah 84041

Book Design by J. Scott Knudsen

Printed and bound in Hong Kong

Library of Congress Cataloging-in-Publication Data

Emerson, Scott, 1959-
    Under the moon and stars / written by Scott Emerson;
  illustrated by Howard Post.
        p.   cm.
    Summary: Tired of being a kid, Andrew leaves home and gets
a job as a cowboy so he can ride the range, eat beans and corn
bread, and sleep under the moon and stars.
    ISBN 0-87905-633-9
    [1. Cowboys—Fiction. 2. Ranch life—Fiction. 3. Family life—
Fiction.]   I. Post, Howard, 1948-   ill. II. Title.
PZ7.E5857Un   1995
[E]—dc20   95–13149
                                              CIP
                                              AC

For Ellen McCaffrey
S.E.

It was eight o'clock and Andrew McAlister was supposed to be asleep.

Instead, he was thinking.

You see, Andrew wasn't tired. He was just tired of being a kid.

He was tired of playing with his little sister. He was tired of cleaning up his room. He was tired of eating meat loaf and mashed potatoes for dinner.

Most of all, he was tired of going to bed at eight o'clock.

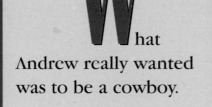

What Andrew really wanted was to be a cowboy.

Cowboys got to wear boots and hats and ride bucking broncs.

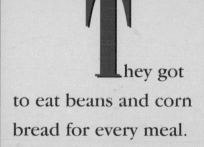

They got
to eat beans and corn
bread for every meal.

They got to sleep in sleeping bags under the moon and stars.

But best of all, cowboys could go to bed anytime they wanted.

After thinking about it for a long time, Andrew knew there was only one thing to do.

"Mom," he said, "I have decided to leave home and become a cowboy."

"Please try not to get your clothes too dirty," said his mother.

The next day, Andrew went to the Bar-T Ranch and asked for a job.

"Kind of short, aren't you?" said Slim, the foreman.

"Not when I'm in the saddle," answered Andrew.

"Where are your boots and hat?" asked Slim.

"I was hoping you might have some I could borrow," said Andrew.

"I suppose you need a horse, too," said Slim as he squinted and pointed to a black stallion standing nearby. "That one tall enough for you?"

"Yes, sir!" answered Andrew.

"You can find a bedroll and some duds over at the bunkhouse," said Slim. "Get a good night's sleep. We hit the trail come sunup."

The next day, Andrew ate a breakfast of beans and corn bread, put on his very own hat and boots, and fell in behind the herd.

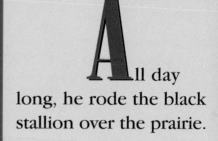

All day long, he rode the black stallion over the prairie.

He practiced hootin' and hollerin'.

He practiced ropin' and brandin'.

He even learned to whistle by putting two fingers between his teeth.

But riding a horse wasn't as easy as it looked, and by the time they made camp, Andrew was tired and hungry, and his mouth was full of dust.

"I could eat ten hamburgers and drink a bucket of soda," he said as he climbed down from the saddle.

"How about a nice heapin' bowl o' beans?" said Slim.

That night, Andrew sang "Home on the Range" with the other cowboys. He learned to play the harmonica. He even stayed up until the moon and stars came out.

As he listened to an owl hooting in the distance, Andrew thought about his stuffed bear, all alone in his bedroom back home.

He hoped his mother remembered to leave the hall light on.

Day after day, Andrew rode the range on his coal black stallion.

Meal after meal, he always had an extra helping of beans and corn bread.

Night after night, he slept in his sleeping bag under the moon and stars.

But sometimes, Andrew wondered what his sister was doing at that very moment.

And more and more often, he found himself wishing his sleeping bag was as soft as his bed at home.

And by the end of the week, he wasn't sure he could eat even one more bean.

That night, while Slim and the other cowboys were snoring like mountain lions, Andrew thought about his life as a cowboy. By the time he fell asleep, he knew there was only one thing to do.

J ust as the sun was coming up, Andrew thanked Slim for the job, said good-bye to the black stallion, and headed toward home.

From that day on, Andrew didn't mind playing with his little sister. He didn't mind cleaning up his room. He was even the first one to the table when his mom made meat loaf and mashed potatoes.

And every night at eight o'clock, he would curl up in his soft, warm bed, hold his stuffed bear close, and drift off to sleep...

...**a**nd sometimes, every so often, Andrew would dream about being a cowboy.

26019